W9-CBT-290

Hairy, Scary, Ordinary

What Is an Adjective?

To Cal and Hannah, two indescribably cool kids
—B.P.C.

To my grandmother Anastasia, the first artist
in our family
—J.P.

adjective: A word that describes a thing, idea, or living being.

Hairy, Scary, Ordinary

What Is an Adjective?

by Brian P. Cleary

illustrated by Jenya Prosmitsky

CAROLRHODA BOOKS, INC. / MINNEAPOLIS

Adjectives are words like hairy,

Scary, cool, and ordinary.

They tell us
things 
are

orange
or
green,

Hot or cold
or in-between,

Leaky, Squeaky, ancient, new,

Easy, breezy, broken, blue.

Adjectives help tell us more,

Like narrow street or favorite store,

Hilly, chilly, fast, and fun,

undercooked and overdone.

They tell us of an
old black boot,

A rainy day,
a wrinkled suit,

A silly teacher, giant hair,

A large cow at the local fair—

Kickballs that are red and rubber,

Spot's clean fur each time you scrub her,

Cold, dark mornings,

hot pink shades,

Young girls drinking lemonades.

That treats
are **yummy**,

shakes are
thick,

And if your
tummy's **calm**
or **sick**.

They're colorful, like mauve and puce,

They help explain, like lean and loose,

99% FAT FREE

Baggy, saggy,

stretchy, strong,

Much too short

or way too long.

Frilly,
silly,

polka-dotted,

single-looped

or

double-knotted.

Words like **spunky,**

rather clunky,

Priceless, nice,

NOT FOR SALE

or downright junky,

Speedy, Spoiled,

Spiffy, Spare,

Thrifty, nifty,

SALE

bronze and bare.

·THE FOOT · MICHELANGEL-TOE·

They **modify** nouns
in ways that help tell us

If
someone's
sincere,

delighted, or **jealous**,

If jackets are
herringbone,
pinstriped, or plaid,

If babies
are

crabby, excited, or glad.

They
tell us
that
shows
are **stupid** or funny,

of books that
are stuffy,
amazing, or punny.

Of looks that are frightening,

dogs that are stray,

of coffee that's black
in a cup
that is gray.

Adjectives help us describe when we're **tired,**

Or say when we're **grumpy,**

or when we are **Wired.**

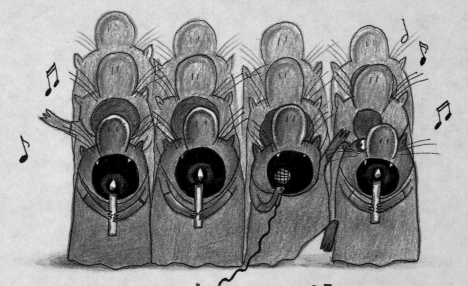

Lopsided, one-sided ball games that bore us,

The sweet, gentle sounds that descend from the chorus,

ABOUT THE AUTHOR & ILLUSTRATOR

BRIAN P. CLEARY is the author of several other picture books,
including A Mink, a Fink, a Skating Rink: What Is a Noun?,
It Looks a Lot Like Reindeer, and Jamaica Sandwich?
He lives in Cleveland.

JENYA PROSMITSKY grew up and studied art in Chisinau, Moldova,
and lives in Minneapolis. Her two cats, Henry and Freddy, were
vital to her illustrations for this book and A Mink, a Fink, a
Skating Rink: What Is a Noun?

Copyright © 2000 by Carolrhoda Books, Inc.

All rights reserved. International copyright secured. No part of this book may be
reproduced, stored in a retrieval system, or transmitted in any form or by any
means—electronic, mechanical, photocopying, recording, or otherwise—without
the prior written permission of Carolrhoda Books, Inc., except for the inclusion
of brief quotations in an acknowledged review.

Carolrhoda Books, Inc., a division of Lerner Publishing Group
241 First Avenue North, Minneapolis, MN 55401 U.S.A.

Library of Congress Cataloging-in-Publication Data

Cleary, Brian P., 1959–
   Hairy, scary, ordinary : what is an adjective? / Brian P. Cleary ;
illustrated by Jenya Prosmitsky.
      p. cm. — (Words are categorical)
   Summary: Rhyming text and illustrations of comical cats present numerous
examples of adjectives, from "hairy, scary, cool, and ordinary" to "tan and tall,"
"funny, frisky, smooth, and small."
   ISBN 1-57505-401-9 (alk. paper)
   1. English language—Adjective—Juvenile literature. [1. English language—
Adjective.] I. Prosmitsky, Jenya, 1974– ill. II. Title. III. Series: Cleary, Brian P.,
1959– Words are categorical.
PE1241.C57 1999   98-32132
428.2—dc21

Printed in Mexico